Farewell to a Fallen Soldier

A letter to my brother

Farewell to a Fallen Soldier

A letter to my brother

Zsaquez Johnson

Farewell to a Fallen Soldier: A letter to my brother

Copyright © 2013 by Zsaquez Johnson

All rights reserved. No portion of this publication may be reproduced, stored in a retrieval system, or transmitted by any means—electronic, mechanical, photocopying, recording, or any other—except for brief quotations in printed reviews, without the prior written permission of the publisher.

> *Editors:* Donna Melillo, Adam Tillinghast, Kayte Middleton, Mollye Vigodsky
> *Cover Design:* Jason Kauffmann / Firelight Interactive / firelightinteractive.com
> *Interior Design:* Rick Soldin / book-comp.com

Indigo River Publishing
3 West Garden Street Ste. 352
Pensacola, FL 32502
www.indigoriverpublishing.com

Ordering Information:
Quantity sales: Special discounts are available on quantity purchases by corporations, associations, and others. For details, contact the publisher at the address above.
Orders by U.S. trade bookstores and wholesalers: Please contact the publisher at the address above.

Printed in the United States of America

Publisher's Cataloging-in-Publication Data is available upon request.
Library of Congress Control Number: 2013949467

Print ISBN: 978-0-9891263-8-0
Digital ISBN: 978-0-9860493-6-1

First Edition

> *With Indigo River Publishing, you can always expect great books, strong voices, and meaningful messages.*
> *Most importantly, you'll always find … words worth reading.*

This book is dedicated to my parents
Dr. Howard Johnson, Sr., and Gloria Johnson.

Thank you for the mental, physical and spiritual nourishment and the priceless life lessons. Thank you for your continued support through all of the joys, sorrows, good times, trials, tribulations as we have stumbled through the darkness. And thank you for your commitment through all the bumps and bruises of life from birth until now. God bless you.

All my love,
Your big girl
Quez

A letter to my brother

Private First Class Howard Johnson II

United States Army 507 Maintenance Company

Killed in action while serving in

Operation Iraqi Freedom

27 January 1982 – 23 March 2003

"For I am persuaded, that neither death, nor life, nor angels, nor principalities, nor powers, nor things present, nor things to come, Nor height, nor depth, nor any other creature, shall be able to separate us from the love of God, which is in Christ Jesus our Lord."

Romans 8:38-39 KJV

Contents

Five Minutes of Wonderful. 1

Tighter than Pantyhose
      Five Sizes Small 11

Did I Do the Right Thing? 25

Why Didn't He Call Today? 45

Life is Forever Better
      Because of You 61

Sleep on, Brother, and Take Your
      Well-Deserved Rest 73

"I never want to forget the sacrifices of so many young men and women. I am so proud it makes me cry. I understand in theory only that war is a part of human nature, but so is love and caring. I wish I could take the families pain away, but I can't. I am committed to loving ALL people, myself and our environment. I am committed to working on my happiness everyday because so many have died for my freedom to live my life. Thank you is not enough, but it is all I have. All my love and respect."

Scott

Five Minutes of Wonderful

Dear Brother,

I'll never forget the day I got the phone call. It was you on the other end of the phone, and just like it was yesterday, I remember you telling me that you had just gotten your orders to be deployed to Iraq. Mentally I was not prepared, and I struggled to control my emotions. I knew deep down in my heart that you were waiting for me to say something profound—maybe you were looking for confirmation that it was okay to go. I've played that conversation back a thousand times in my mind. I tried to assure you that everything was going to be okay, but that wasn't enough. You were waiting for me to say

Farewell to a

something to comfort you, and I feel like I never gave you the comfort you needed. But what's a big sister to say when her little brother gets orders to leave the country?

I was overwhelmed with mixed emotions. Should I feel happy that you're getting a chance to see another part of the world? Or should I feel sad that my little brother is going to the front lines? All of a sudden, it occurred to me that you needed my strength more than you had ever needed it in your life. I was the problem solver, and here was a situation that I had no control over. There were no phone calls to make to remedy this. Uncle Sam demanded you to follow the orders. Completely unaware of the details of how you had prepared or what you would be facing, I somehow knew you were ready. At that moment, you sounded so brave and fearless, and I was the one that was comforted by a serene and peaceful spirit dwelling within you.

Fallen Soldier

I kept telling you, "You're coming back, and I'm going to give you the biggest boss party that Mobile has ever seen." Later, I kept telling myself the same thing. And I kept myself occupied with thoughts of you coming home, rather than thoughts of you in a war zone—thoughts of the *inexperienced* you in a war zone. I mean, you had just graduated from high school in May.

In June, you signed up to join the United States Army. Two months later, I remember going to your graduation from basic training. This was too fast, too soon. Despite all that happened so quickly, Daddy kept saying, "I'm peacock proud and hyena happy of my boy." Everybody wanted to go to the graduation. As always, though, we were running late. I was driving Grandma, Aunt Ruth, Aunt Monica, and Cousin Niesha; and we were behind the Sequoia, which your sister Selle was driving. I got comfortable around 100 and laid down on it. At one point, a

Farewell to a

state trooper rode up on my left side. I still don't know how I didn't get a speeding ticket. Aunt Ruth looked out the window at the state trooper and she said, "Quez, the kojack with the Kodak got a grip on you." We all laughed. When we stopped for gas, I remember Uncle Charles said, "Can you guys please slow down? My van can't go that fast!" Once we reached the facility where the graduation was being held, we were seated and patiently waited for the ceremony to begin. Proud expressions of gladness and shining smiles beamed from all of us. Momma and Daddy looked in the crowd of graduates and searched until they spotted you. Daddy said, "There goes my boy." Momma was calling your name, taking pictures and smiling saying, "Look at my boy! My boy made it from basic training!" They knew basic training wasn't easy, and they were so proud, not just because you got through, but more importantly of the man you were becoming.

Fallen Soldier

From basic training you went to do your MOS (Military Occupational Specialty) in Virginia. Upon completion, you were ordered to be stationed in Fort Hood, Texas. Remember when you told me how much you loved El Paso and how much you loved being a soldier? Remember when you told me you found a church that you liked? You said the pastor of the church in El Paso reminded you of Daddy, and you were thinking about joining under Watch Care so you could keep your membership here at Truevine. After much persistent prayer and careful consideration, you joined and offered your services as a percussionist. You grew to love your new church family as well. I watched you grow and blossom and mature mentally, spiritually, and physically.

I did not know, nor did the thought ever cross my mind, that I would never see you again. I never got a chance to tell you how proud of you I was.

Farewell to a Fallen Soldier

I never got a chance to tell you just how very much I LOVE YOU.

Private First Class Howard Johnson II, of the United States Army 507 Maintenance Company, you will always be regarded by me as a brave, courageous, and honorable young man—a trusted confidant, friend, and brother. You were, and always will be, my HERO.

It was a privilege to have had five minutes of wonderful with you rather than a life time of nothing special. You had your five minutes of wonderful, and you will go down in the history as the first fallen soldier in the Iraq War from the state of Alabama, and the city of Mobile. You were one of the eleven who made the ultimate sacrifice that day.

"To the Johnson Family: Your son was a funny young man who can make you laugh so hard unexpectedly. When you are a soldier in the military, the soldiers you serve with becomes your sister or brother. Johnson was like a little brother, always sweet and respectful. My heart went out to Johnson's family because I knew how much he loved his family. To drive from Texas to Alabama in his beige Grand Marquis reminds me of the saying 'When you raise your kids right they always come home to visit.' I miss him so much. Johnson and Sloan—two young soldiers who I will always remember."

Selena

Tighter than Pantyhose Five Sizes Small

Daddy wanted a boy so bad. He thought I was going to be a boy, but I wasn't. Then when Momma was expecting for the second time, Daddy just *knew* it was going to be a boy, but it wasn't that time either. It was the arrival of our sister Geiselle LaVonne. He loved both of us very much, but Daddy always dreamed of having a boy someday.

Finally, it happened. When the news of our expecting Mother was spread, Daddy was so happy he skipped around like a school boy. When it was time for you to be born, we were elated. I remember the day you came home from the hospital. Selle and I were turning flips and popping our fingers. When we heard them pull up in the yard, our faces were glued to the window as Daddy opened the car door for Momma, and they proceeded to come in the house. It seemed like they had you wrapped in about 15 blankets.

When they took the last blanket from around you, there you were—the face of our only brother. Your complexion was like that of our mother. Your face was handsomely rounded, and your eyes were dancing green. Selle waved her hand in front of your eyes, but you did not blink. She told Daddy, "I think they gave you the wrong baby. He's blind. Take him back to the hospital." You looked like a precious lump of sugar to me—so innocent and unassuming. I knew the moment I laid eyes on you that you and I would be fast friends.

Momma and Daddy were always so busy working at the church; I was like a second mother to you. I did a lot of brother-sitting while you were growing up, and I loved every minute of it. I loved

Fallen Soldier

you as if you were my own. When I was a young teenager, Momma had to go to California for a while. Daddy went to Texas for two weeks for a preacher's convention, and I was left to care for you and Selle in their absence. Daddy gave us the keys to Momma's car, a 1982 Lincoln Mark IV, which he had just purchased as a gift for Momma when you were born. He also gave us $200 cash and the checkbook. That was an interesting couple of weeks. I drove you to the park, took you to Grandma's house, and even took you grocery shopping with me. By the time Momma came back, you wouldn't even go to her. You always wanted me.

You and I were so close. We went everywhere and did everything together. We were jammed up and honey tight, and tighter than pantyhose five sizes small. We had a genuine, unique, and original brother-sister relationship. We were almost inseparable. On Sundays, when I played the piano,

Farewell to a

you sat beside me on the piano stool. When you fell asleep, I laid you across my lap and continued to play. You learned to play the drums when you were only three years old, and Daddy bought you your own set that Christmas. Every day when you came home, you told me you heard a new beat and asked me to play the piano, and you accompanied me with the drums.

Remember when it was time for me to go off to college? You kicked, hollered, screamed, and cried, "Please don't go! Don't leave me!" After that pitiful display of sorrow, Daddy told me I couldn't go. He simply said, "That boy is taking your going off to college too hard. You need to go to Mobile College until that boy gets a little older." I tried reasoning with you because I really wanted to go away to college. I promised to come home often and send you money, but you wouldn't hear of it. You insisted that I stay.

After my attendance at Mobile College, I moved to Fort Lauderdale, Florida. That was hard on you

Fallen Soldier

too. The only way you let me go was because I promised to call you every day. Remember our deal? You said, "If I let you go, you better call me every day. If you don't, I'm gonna make you come back home." Well I kept my word. I called you every day at the exact same time, and you were always sitting by the phone waiting for my call. Remember how I would always tell you I loved you and ask how you were doing? You would always say, "Come get me. I want to go with you!" Or, "Please come home right now! Please come home! Selle hits me every day. Momma is crying because she has to cook and clean the house now that you are gone, and Daddy is crying now because now he has to eat her cooking. Come home please!" Now I know it wasn't that bad, but you sure knew how to guilt trip me! How I missed you and so looked forward to coming home to see you back then.

Remember how you would never let me speak to Momma and Daddy? You would always say they were gone to a prayer meeting and laugh. You always knew how to reduce me to tears with your request for me to come home in that pitiful trembling voice. I loved to hear your voice when I called. I wanted to know how you were doing in school, if you had any new friends, and what your plans were for the weekend. I wanted to know if anyone was bothering you—if I needed to go to your school and grab someone because they were messing with you. After all, we were basically super-glued together.

Remember when you came to Fort Lauderdale to visit me for the summer as you got older? I took you to work with me at the funeral home every day. Mr. Boyd, the owner of the funeral home, thought you were the most handsome boy he had ever seen and treated you like a grandson. Just like Daddy, he fell in love with you instantly. He often passed the time of day teasing you, claiming that you were my son and not my brother. He took you shopping,

Fallen Soldier

bought you many suits of clothes, and had you working funerals. You were the youngest, cutest funeral attendant that anyone had ever seen. He always had you standing next to the widow with one arm around her, holding a box of tissues in the other hand, and gently whispering in the ear of the bereaved, "Ask God for strength."

Everywhere we went, people wanted to keep you. They thought you were so cute and adorable; you got more hugs and kisses than a newborn baby. We went to the beach and the movies—and everywhere we went, people wanted you to do commercials and be a movie star. I remember calling Momma and Daddy, telling them that they wanted you to be in the movies. It was so funny—Momma started calculating your paycheck, and Daddy packed and headed to Fort Lauderdale. Obviously it never happened, but it was fun to dream.

Speaking of Momma and Daddy, remember the time we went to Dad's friend's cabin on the lake? Daddy was trying to teach us all how to cast the line into the water to catch the fish. When he gave you the fishing pole, you cast the line as hard as you could. Almost immediately, you felt a tug; you were so excited! You started yelling, "I got one! I got one!" and started pulling as hard as you could. All of a sudden, Momma started screaming. That's when we realized you had caught Momma's hair, not a fish! We were happy it was just her hair and she wasn't hurt. Even with that small incident, we still had such a great time together as a family.

Cousin Lisa has a video of you at Derrick's 5th birthday party, and you were the only one that showed up in a 3-piece suit. And once you started dancing, all the kids surrounded you chanting "Go Junior; go Junior!" Even at a young age, you had a magnetic personality that made everyone like you and want to be around you.

I remember the first day we moved to the new house in Skywood in 1991. Al welcomed us to the neighborhood and became your best friend. Y'all went to school together, played together, double dated together, and went everywhere together. Al really misses you. He still comes by my house to see me, and we still eat oysters on the patio and talk about the club that you and he wanted together. He lives in Birmingham now, but he comes by to see me as often as he can.

You were always so friendly. Most folks bring home stray cats or dogs—you brought home stray people. You kept Momma in the kitchen cooking and serving your strays, and you kept Daddy wondering who you were going to bring home next. You never met a stranger. Even after I moved back to Mobile, you often came to my house and knocked on the door. And as I came to answer the door, I could hear you say, "Come on in and eat with us. My sister has already cooked." Many times, you woke me up in the middle of the night telling me that you had "important news" for me. Instead, you'd sit on the foot of my bed and ask me to fry oysters and fish at 2:00 in the morning. A lot of times, I wanted to give you a buck fifty and slap the top of your head; but as your big sister, I got up and did it anyway.

That's just the kind of person you were. Ever since you were little, you talked to everyone anywhere you went. You were kind and compassionate to everyone. When we were kids, Dad always told us to be friendly to our fellow man. He reminded us all the time, "If we want to be a friend, we must show ourselves friendly." We couldn't go into the church and let anyone know we were upset or mad. We always had to be friendly and talkative. We were expected to fellowship, hug people, and shake hands with people. I think this is why you were always so giving and kind to everyone. It's just the way you were from a very early age.

You always looked for ways to help people—whether it was washing someone's clothes, feeding them, or even helping them fill out an application. You even had *us* helping with these things. It was just the spirit you had.

As much as you bugged me at times, I miss all the time we spent together as you were growing up. We were best of friends; I miss you more than words can say.

"You touched the lives of so many people … your beautiful smile & mannerism shown to others will be cherished forever … We miss & love you still today … your memories live on … May you continue to rest in peace …"

Sonja

Did I Do the Right Thing?

Daddy still talks about you all the time, and he's never anything but proud. He likes to reminisce about the good times he shared with you. When you were only three years old, Daddy took you to the Mobile District Sunlight Association. He loved how you would always carry a Bible, just like he did. You used to sit and stare at your open Bible, appearing to be reading even though you couldn't at the time. People marveled, thinking you were actually studying your Scriptures.

You and Daddy had so many wonderful experiences together. He loves to tell of the day he was taking you to daycare at the age of three, and you looked up and asked him if you could stay with

Farewell to a

him that day. Daddy said, "You know, I have a lot to do today." Not to be denied, you asked, "What do you have to do?" And he replied, "Go to the bank, go to the hospital, make house calls, check on the sick, and attend the Baptist Ministers meeting." Your reply was, "Take me on to the daycare. I don't want to be a preacher; he have too much to do." Daddy shared your sentiments with the church, and Deacon Lee Perkins replied, "I'm on Junior's side; I don't wanna be no preacher either."

When you were four years old, you asked Daddy if you could fly to Dallas, Texas, to go the National Baptist Convention with him. This is when you experienced your first flight by way of Delta Airlines—and what a flight it was! What an exciting experience for a four-year-old little boy! He said you were smiling from ear to ear. While boarding the plane, you yelled to us, clinging to Daddy with one hand, and waving to us with the other. As the plane

Fallen Soldier

slowly rolled down the bumpy runway, you called out, "Daddy, we are crashing!" "No, baby, we are not crashing," Daddy responded. Climbing steadily toward a comfortable flying altitude, the plane suddenly made alarming rough-scratching sounds, and you said, "Daddy, are we crashing?" He replied, "No, son, we are not crashing." You said, "I wish we were crashing!" A senior passenger looked at you and said, "I don't think you want to crash; we all might be killed." Daddy said it took some doing, but the two of them finally convinced you that a plane crash was *not* a good thing to experience.

A smile comes to Daddy's face when he thinks of all of us driving to Pittsburg, Pennsylvania, for another National Baptist Convention. The St. Louis Cardinals were visiting the Pittsburg Pirates. You were only about five years old, but you kept pleading with Daddy to take you to the game. You finally won him over, and the two of you walked from the hotel

Farewell to a

to the ballpark. Your eyes glowed and beamed as you stepped into that stadium. As you passed by the broadcasting booth, Jack Buch invited you for a quick tour and presented you with an autographed baseball which we kept for you until the house burned down. Daddy told me that he believes that was one of the happiest moments of your life.

Remember when you always wanted to wear Daddy's socks and neckties rather than your own? You wanted to use Daddy's deodorant, eat his Tic Tacs, and use everything else that belonged to him. So many people started calling you "Junior," "Little Preacher," "Junior Man," "Joe Bob," and "Muffin."

Then there was the day at the Alabama State Women's Convention when you were dressed in your white suit, just like Daddy, standing with your Bible open. Preachers were going to him asking for a telephone number so they could get that "little preacher" to come and preach for them. Daddy

Fallen Soldier

explained to them that you were not a preacher—
that you were his son. You loved all the attention.

You were four years old when Daddy took you
hunting for the first time. You enjoyed the hunting
experience so much that Daddy bought you a BB
gun and taught you how to use it. He taught you
safety rules and all the pros and cons of hunting. You
learned quickly and you learned well.

For Daddy, you were not only his son, but his
best friend. You and Daddy traveled together, going
fishing and hunting, and Daddy even went to Boy
Scout camp with you. He still beams with excitement
when he talks about the first deer you killed at the
age of ten. That day, you were the only one to kill a
deer; you teased the group by saying, "I fed you guys
today." Remember the "ritual" that the hunters had?
If someone missed a deer, another hunter would
cut his shirttail. The day you got your first deer, you
borrowed Daddy's knife to cut his shirttail after *he*

missed a deer. The guys in the hunting club thought it was so funny, and you stole the show like always.

Daddy loves to talk about how you became so close to the guys in the hunting club and how you loved to tease them. You always carried your own ammunition, knife, and gun. All of the guys were amazed to see how skilled you were. Daddy fondly remembers the day you refused to fire at moving bushes and could not shoot when the deer came out too quickly. The guys complained about you not killing the deer. You asked Daddy, "Did I do the right thing? I didn't shoot because I only saw bushes moving. I didn't want to shoot a man or a dog. Did I do right?" Daddy replied, "I'm proud of you, son. It's better to be safe than sorry."

Then there was the time that you phoned Daddy when he was on a trip to the National Convention in Saginaw, Michigan, to inform him that you had shot the big dog in the foot because he

Fallen Soldier

was killing one of the little dogs. Again, you said, "Did I do the right thing?" Dad said, "You the man of the house, and I am way up here in Michigan. I am proud of your courage to make a good decision."

I know these situations helped create the man you became. They taught you to use caution in your decisions and to think about how the decisions you made affected other people. It was a priceless life lesson and made you a better decision-maker in life.

Remember your last hunt together? Daddy wanted you to kill a deer, and everyone was gathering for a second hunt that night. He couldn't go fast enough, so he said he wanted you to go on with them and get you one of the good stands so you could kill a deer. You said to him, "I'm not leaving you if I never kill another deer." You didn't run off and leave him when he couldn't keep up. You sat him on your shoulders and carried him, saying, "You are my daddy.

Farewell to a

I'm taking care of you." Daddy had never been so proud to have you for a son.

Well, little brother, you have been updated on many enjoyable moments with Dad, but there is much more to come. Daddy also began teaching you to drive at the age of four. By the time you were seven, you could handle a vehicle with manly skills. Remember when you were eight, and Daddy had given you permission to drive around the church yard while he was taking a shower? The police saw you driving and came over, thinking you were actually stealing the car. You screamed, "I ain't doin' nothing wrong! My daddy is in the church, and this is his car!" The police came in and told Daddy you were too young to drive, even on private property. Yes, you and Daddy were a great team.

Daddy loves us all, but you were the joy of his life, being his only son. Your following him around was a treasured pleasure for Daddy. Now that you're

Fallen Soldier

gone, your nephew Zuke is Daddy's new road buddy. They go everywhere together—fishing, hunting, church, the doctor—everywhere, just like you and Daddy used to.

You loved being with Daddy. He recalls that when he would drop you off at our Mawmaw's house in the morning, you would always ask her if the grits and eggs was ready. When Daddy would get ready to leave, you would say, "Don't be so long picking me up." And he would always respond, "I'll get back as soon as I can."

Daddy and I weren't the only ones who were in love with you. Aunt Saluda and Sister McCance used to bring you a dollar bill every Sunday morning, and Deacon Archibald would let you drive his car to pick up members on Sunday mornings. You always loved to do things for children and the elderly, putting toys together at Christmas, going to the store, and reading the Bible as we listened. Daddy further recalls some scary moments with you—like the Sunday morning you slipped and fell down the stairs at the old Truevine, hurting your bottom and, as a result, having to be taken to Providence Hospital for emergency room treatment. Or the day when you were leaning on the car door and it flew open and you were clinging to the armrest swinging on the door. Daddy managed to slow the car down and stop without throwing you out into the traffic. It was scary, but fortunately it ended well.

Remember your graduation day from high school and how Daddy comforted you as you wept after graduation exercises were over because many of you would not see each other anymore? Daddy said to you, "Son, it's like moving away from a neighborhood—some friends you see again, and some you never see anymore. But you must go on to a higher level." Again, this showed your caring personality and how you always thought of others.

Fallen Soldier

When you enlisted in the military, remember how proud Daddy was to look upon you decked out so neat and fit in your Army greens? Shirt neatly tucked in your pants, shoe strings tightly tied, and your belt properly placed—what a real joy it was to look upon a well-groomed, mature Army soldier. The trip to your graduation exercise following your basic training was a privilege. But for Daddy, the trip was a physical challenge. None of us knew how he kept his pain and discomfort from us all. He was in the early stages of kidney failure then, but we knew nothing of it.

When basic training was over, off you went to learn advanced skills. It seemed that you were gone so long, but finally the day came for you to come home from Virginia—and my, what a day! You had 18 days before you went off to your next assignment, and that day came far too soon. But then, that's life … and life is sometimes pleasant and sometimes

Farewell to a

not-so-pleasant—sometimes happy, and sometimes not-so-happy. But life must go on.

The original plan was for you to fly from New Orleans to where you were to be stationed at Fort Bliss in El Paso, Texas. Instead, Daddy took you to Daphne, Alabama, and co-signed for a 1999 Mercury Grand Marquis. We all knew you were getting a car, but it was a surprise for you. Oh how you loved that car! (Momma still has it today.) Daddy had some concerns about you driving to the base all alone, but you assured him you could do it. So Daddy gave in and allowed you to go by yourself. He spoke with you all through the day and night until you arrived there safely. Thank God for your safe arrival!

We didn't know it then, but later Daddy revealed for the first time his deep sorrow and fear over seeing you for the last time. He thought that you would be grieving over his demise because he was so sick and told no one. He was so ill.

Fallen Soldier

We were so grateful to see you several times while you were stationed in Fort Bliss. Remember the last time you came home before you were deployed? Daddy was supposed to pick you up from the airport in New Orleans, but he was too sick to drive by himself. Remember that Pastor Sandy McQueen drove Daddy to pick you up? Daddy was so sick, but none of us realized how serious it was. They got to the airport just as you walked through the door. You drove Daddy and Pastor McQueen back to Mobile.

You were home for two weeks, and of course that time passed too quickly. The whole time that you were home, Daddy says he wrestled with the pain of how you would handle his death. Would the Red Cross be able to get word to you in time to get you to his funeral? How would you react to the news? What would you say? What would you do? Daddy says he actually prayed to God for His strength for you

Farewell to a

to deal with *his* death, not realizing that it was our family who would need to be strengthened.

The day you were preparing to head back to Texas for the last time, I stopped by the house to say goodbye to you. I wanted to take you to the airport myself, but there were too many families coming to the funeral home to make arrangements that day. I just couldn't take off from work. You and I were giving each other high-fives and talking about the party I was gonna throw you when you came home.

Momma was not feeling well that November morning, so she didn't ride to New Orleans with you and Daddy. Before you left, you hugged Momma as if hugging was going out of style. Daddy said he knew something was going to happen, but he wasn't sure what. He knew he was sick, but he didn't know what it was at the time. He said he really didn't feel like driving to the airport, but he knew you had to get back to the base on time. You asked Daddy to

Fallen Soldier

take you to see Aunt Ruby, who was ill, just so you could say goodbye to her. Daddy said he felt that day that you guys were spending your last day together. Remember when you hugged your Aunt Ruby? She kissed you on your forehead, you eased into the passenger seat, and you turned and waived to Aunt Ruby as long as you could see her. Daddy asked you if you wanted to drive, but you surprisingly said, "You drive, Daddy," and you slipped off into a peaceful sleep. Daddy says that as he watched you sleep, a feeling came over him, ever stronger, that you would not see him alive again.

Remember you woke up when you were about halfway to New Orleans? You and Daddy talked about your relationship with God, and you assured him that you were good with God. As you arrived at the airport in good time, Daddy's heart was heavy with grief. He knew he was seeing you for the last time. He thought the next time you would see him,

Farewell to a Fallen Soldier

he would be in his going-home casket. You guys hugged, kissed, and waved goodbye as you walked in to the airport. Daddy just sat in his car across the street and prayed and cried for a short period of time. He said the trip back home was one of the longest of his life. Several times he even had to stop. The burden of grief was so heavy, and the pain of death was almost unbearable.

You and Daddy were so close. You attached yourself to him when I moved to Florida. You would even go "up the country," as Daddy called it, to Jackson, Alabama to see all of Daddy's family for Thanksgiving every year. You were like a best friend to him. He misses you so much … we all do.

"You probably don't remember me, but I am the little girl from McGill that Howard did the honor of escorting to two dances while we were in high school. I just want to let you know that he is truly loved and missed, and I know he is an angel looking down upon us. I remember the Eulogy from his funeral where Mr. Johnson talked about a Prince returning home; nothing could be more true than those words."

Walkitria

Why Didn't He Call Today?

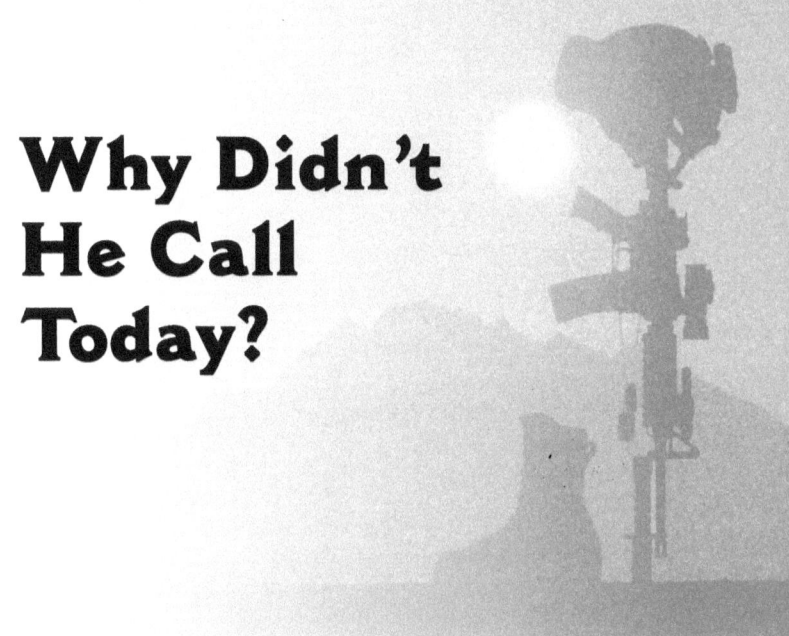

You grew up to be an outstanding young man. I was so proud of you. Growing up, we were taught that family was everything, and you and I were as close as family could be. I guess that's why I missed you even more when you were in Iraq.

I could never forget all those letters that you sent me while you were there, including those with $25 checks that you sent me, telling me it was my "ice cream money." I was so proud of your letters that I showed them to everybody. And I felt so loved by you to be in the midst of a war zone and yet you still found time to write me and call me every day. After all, we had talked every day since I left for college so many years before.

Farewell to a

Rice, my boss at the funeral home, used to always ask me why I was on the phone all the time. I told him, "My brother is in Iraq. Every time he calls, I'm gonna talk to him!" Then he'd say, "That boy can't be in Iraq. How is he able to call you every day?" Nobody believed you called me every day; but you did. By the way, I'm still waiting for that Crown Liquor you promised me. Every time I look at it, or think about it, or see it on TV, I think about you.

You loved to describe what it was like in Iraq. You told me how beautiful the country was—it wasn't only what they showed us on TV back here in the States. You told me about the beautiful scenery, about the men in your company, and just life in general. You always made me pass on messages to the rest of the family too.

I started putting together a care package for you with all your favorite snacks—Doritos, Cheetos, and Snickers bars. When people found out I was sending

Fallen Soldier

you a package, they started making contributions to the box as well. There was so much stuff that I finally had to go get a bigger box.

I was worried and concerned that two days had gone by, and I hadn't heard from you. I asked Momma and Daddy if they had heard from you, and I remember Daddy saying, "That boy is fighting a war. He can't talk on the telephone." Later, when I saw on the news that your company was involved in an ambush, my immediate thought was, "Lord, take care of my brother." When we didn't hear anything immediately, I thought to myself, "No news is good news." But then I thought, "Why didn't he call today? Every day—he calls every day." Shortly after though, my worst fears were confirmed.

The day before I was going to tape the box shut and ship it to you, there was a government vehicle parked outside Momma and Daddy's house. Daddy picked up your niece Cooter from school that day and came straight home. As he approached the driveway, he saw the vehicle parked in front of the house. He told Cooter to go in the house. They got out of the car and asked Daddy, "Are you Mr. Johnson?" Sadly, he replied, "Yes, I am." He walked up the driveway and invited the government officials inside. He told the government officials that he already knew what they were there to say, for he saw it in a dream. Once inside, he invited them to sit on the sofa, and they graciously accepted. As he sat down, the news he had been dreading since we saw the news reports were confirmed: you were gone. Daddy kept the news of your untimely demise to himself until he could get us all together to tell us.

I remember he came by my job at the funeral home that day and insisted that I come home with him. He said that he wanted to talk to me—that he needed me to come by the house after work. I said, "Why? I'm so tired. Can this wait until tomorrow?"

Fallen Soldier

He said, "I need you to come today." I didn't want to, but I reluctantly agreed. I didn't know that he had called my sister and my mother already and told them the same thing.

When I got to the house, everyone was seated, and we were waiting for Daddy to come out of his room. I knew something was wrong; I just didn't know what. I remember Momma calling on the telephone and asking why Daddy wanted us to come home. She explained that she was delayed, but she'd be there shortly. We were all seated in the den, wondering what Daddy wanted. I called to him and said, "Daddy, what's wrong? Are you okay?" He opened the door to his room. I can still picture him coming down the hall, walking very slowly. When he reached the den, with his head hung down, he calmly said in a broken voice, "Howard is no longer with us."

Even when he said that, I didn't imagine that you were gone. It just didn't register with me. I kept

Farewell to a

saying, "What do you mean?" I cried out, "Daddy, what are you talking about? I just talked to that boy a few days ago. I'm sending him a box tomorrow." He repeated it again, "Howard is no longer with us; he is gone." After about the seventh time he said it, it finally started to sink in. My worst fears had come to pass—you had perished in Operation Iraqi Freedom.

In disbelief, I cried out, "No! No! No! He can't be gone!" I screamed your name over and over and over and fell to my knees. "He can't be!" I screamed. "Daddy, no!" At that point, I was dead, just not buried. I screamed, moaned, and groaned. I did so for such a long time, I found myself being contained by our father. I remember apologizing to him for my outburst. My sister who said she had already saw it in a dream, sat there in disbelief. My daughter was immediately deeply saddened and wept uncontrollably, for you were her only uncle, Uncle Junior—the only one she let call her Cooter.

Fallen Soldier

The news of your passing lacerated my heart and caused it to bleed open with sorrow. It shook and shattered my soul. As my knees weakened, I became breathless, and my heart started skipping beats, for it was beyond comprehension how this could have happened. I was overcome with an overwhelming sense of sorrow, and I was deeply saddened. It was an indescribable, unspeakable, unexplainable sadness that I shall never forget. There is no song; there are no words; there is no place to express how I really felt inside. I was just drinking from my saucer because my cup overflowed.

You were the closest person to me. We were advisors to each other. We talked and problematically solutionized situations, trials, and tribulations, circumstances that presented themselves to us we always shared our hopes, our dreams, ambitions, plans, and secrets. My only brother, my God, this can't be true! I prayed, "Lord, have mercy, Father, 'cause mercy suits my case. Dear God, don't let my heart hurt so bad!" I cried out. Momma and Daddy were broken beyond repair.

As we had anticipated your arrival in birth, likewise we did as well in your death. At that moment, I felt weak in my knees. In my mind, I envisioned you as last I saw you—with a great big smile, a silly grin, and your giant walk. Much to our dismay, the official notice was relayed indicating that your remains were deemed unviewable. I thought to myself, "I don't care. Just get him home, and get him home now. Right now." You know, in my reflection, it seemed like it took them so long to get you home. Those government officials were moving and shaking, shucking and jiving, and fumbling around like a blind dog in a meat house.

The government officials came from Washington, DC, with published reports of exactly what happened on that fateful day. They said that

Fallen Soldier

someone in your convoy had run out of fuel. With the 507 being a maintenance and supply company, the commander ordered half of the convoy to go back and re-fuel the military vehicle. Once the vehicle was re-fueled, they were supposed to meet up at a checkpoint. However, there was a sandstorm which caused the GPS to malfunction. Once the convoy had crossed the Euphrates, they realized they were in enemy territory. They tried to turn back, but it was too late. Iraqis opened fire and ambushed the 507 maintenance company. You and 10 other people lost their lives. The Iraqis took many of the bodies, but they couldn't get yours. You were pinned in the driver's seat. Eventually, the Marines fought their way up to you and rescued your body. They said that you died instantly. Once your body was taken from the military vehicle, it was taken to Germany, and from there it was taken to Dover, DE. From there, it was brought home to Mobile, AL. You were escorted

Farewell to a

by Major Robert Tally, our cousin. As the flight descended into Mobile, the pilot announced that they were carrying a fallen soldier on the plane. The plane broke out into a thunderous applause. Below is an eyewitness account of what happened on the plane:

"I want to tell you of an experience I had last night flying home from Atlanta. The pilot came on the intercom and went through the usual announcements telling us that 'we're just east of Montgomery cruising at 28,000 feet' and 'you've picked a beautiful night for flying, just look at the gorgeous southern sunset out of the right side of the plane.'"

He then, however said this: 'Please bear with me as I deviate from the script, but I want you all to know that simply by coincidence you have been granted both the privilege and honor of escorting the body of Army PFC Howard Johnson, Jr. home tonight. PFC Johnson was killed in Iraq defending the freedoms we

Fallen Soldier

all enjoy, and fighting to extend those freedoms to the people of Iraq. We are also accompanied by PFC Johnson's cousin, Marine Major Talley, who has been chosen by the family to escort PFC Johnson home. Semper Fi!'

The plane quickly became very quiet but soon erupted in thunderous applause that lasted for several minutes. It was quite moving, to say the least. As I sat there thinking about what the pilot had said, and visualizing PFC Johnson's dead body riding below me in the belly of that plane, I noticed a couple of things. Two rows in front of me sat a father holding his daughter, an infant, and they were practicing 'ma-ma' and in the row behind me was another young boy, probably 2 or so, learning to count to 10. Now obviously both are too young to realize we're at war, or that one of our dead was with us, but it made me think, and this is the point: These warriors, mostly young, all volunteers, everyday are prepared to give

Farewell to a

their lives for our future, for a safer, more secure future for people they don't even know, all based on the principle that fighting and dying for this country is worth it. You all know and agree with this, but not everyone does, so I would ask that if you meet anyone that's not 'on board' with this philosophy, i.e. the protesters, that you 'correct the situation.'

By the way, the flight ended with all of us deplaning only to line the windows of the gate house to watch PFC Johnson's body, draped in the American flag, be rolled out of the plane and into a waiting hearse that was surrounded by his family members. Please pray that our soldiers' sight is acute, their aim is true, and that as many come home as God can spare."

Meanwhile, we all waited to meet you at the airport. As your casket was unloaded from the plane,

Fallen Soldier

we saw that it was draped with the American Flag. It was all so official, but very respectful at the same time. There were military officials standing at attention as they carried you from the plane. Our family all stood by as they reverently loaded you into a hearse and sent you on to the funeral home. Other soldiers come home every day, and I see them embrace their family and loved ones. You came home in a casket. I thought, "No way! How can this be fair?"

Your death left a big void in our family. You were the only boy—you were the baby. It was so unexpected and tragic and sad to know that you were gone. We were so glad to have a brother when you were born; but all of a sudden, we lost our only brother. The fact that you were taken away tragically and so suddenly made it even worse. You were the light of everyone's life. You were the life of the party—the one who made us all laugh. That void cannot be filled.

"Hello my name is Kimberly, and I served with Johnson. We were both stationed at Ft. Bliss and had to go to war together. Johnson was my friend and co-worker; he had a heart of gold and always wore a smile on his face. I will always remember and love him. Rest in Peace, troop."

Kimberly

Life is Forever Better Because of You

You were robbed. And the thing that bothers me the most is that no one was ever arrested for the robbery. You didn't get a chance to court a girl proper or graduate from college. You didn't get a chance to have a formal wedding, witness the birth of your children, or spoil your grandchildren. You missed family trips and outings, birthdays, anniversaries, Valentine's Day, Easters, Thanksgivings, and Christmases. You have missed Sunday dinners, special occasions, and celebrations. Once again, I keep thinking, "It's just not fair!"

And then, "How dare I question God!" I mean, I thought about questioning Him, but He was not on trial. And I am no prosecutor. I perished the thought

Farewell to a

of pressing charges—accusing Him and cross-examining God in my mental courtroom. I had been taught at an early age to fear God, trust Him, and obey His Word, for He is the Supreme Master and Grand Chancellor of the universe. How dare I stray from my childhood teachings? Instead of putting God on trial, I cried, I stomped, I hollered, and I prayed for mercy, for I felt that it suited my case at the time.

Before you left for Iraq, I promised to give you the biggest coming home party Mobile had ever seen. After you passed, I remembered the welcome home party I had promised you, and I kept my word. Since I worked at a funeral home, it was only natural that I ask Daddy to allow me to take care of all the details of your home going service. Immediately I went to work planning your funeral—your welcome home party.

What a funeral you had! Headlines in the newspapers read, "First fallen from the state of Alabama, PFC Howard Johnson II from the

Fallen Soldier

507 Maintenance Company." Countless people attended your funeral, honoring your memory and remembering the impact you had on their lives. For most it was a final tribute to a man they truly loved. From the time you were a little boy, you affected those around you. Your interaction with others made a lasting impression—whether it be fellow hunters or the "strays" you brought home to feed. Comments from so many who were there attested to your warmth and concern for others. It made me so proud to hear them speak so well of you!

Pastor Onnie Kirk and much of your church family from El Paso came to your funeral by the bus load, and some even flew by airplane. The pastor spoke very highly of you, both as a member of their church and about your ministering in their services by playing the drums. Pastor Kirk related to us the first time you came into his office, wanting to play the drums. He asked you if you knew Jesus. You told him

Farewell to a

He was your Savior, so Pastor Kirk asked you to read John 3:16 and tell him what it meant. You said, "It's telling me Momma loves me, Daddy loves me, but God loves me more." Dr. Kirk said you were hired right then and there because he could look at you and tell you were raised right.

People came from all corners of the world: military officials, dignitaries, senators, the governor, the Mayor, city officials, your Leflore High School classmates, and Congressman Joe Bonner served as your Master of Ceremony. Your funeral service was broadcasted on national TV, as well as in England and Germany. The Early Show, Good Morning America, CNN, *USA Today*, and newspapers from England and Germany requested interviews.

Fallen Soldier

No one had ever seen a funeral procession like yours before. As we got into the limousine, there was nothing but cars as far as the eye could see—more than 200 cars were in that procession. We were escorted by the Mobile Police Department, and Interstate 65 was shut down all the way until we reached the church exit. There was no one on the interstate but the funeral procession. As we got off the interstate and approached the street to the church, there were people lined up as far as the eye could see on the sides of the street waving the American flag. When we reached the church, we were astounded by the number of cars. They were parked as far as three miles away from the church. As we got out of the car and started to line up for the procession, I could not believe my eyes—there were so many people. We gave you top billing, and we packed the house at your funeral; it was standing room only. There was no room—not even for a fly or a mosquito. It was a service fit for a prince.

Your home-going was a thing of beauty. What a beautiful casket you lay in. It was gold and was adorned with a huge display of fresh roses. Flowers, cards, resolutions, telegrams, lovely and sincere expressions of condolences, and numerous exhibitions and suggestions of sympathetic gestures were piled high near your casket.

The atmosphere was one of blessing and thankfulness, accompanied by unbearable sadness and grief. We sat quietly and tearfully among the mourners. Instead of traditional black, we were dressed patriotically in the old red, white, and blue. Daddy did an awesome job in delivering your eulogy. As he spoke, we clung to his every word. I rest assured with the highest degree of certainty that God was there, and His presence was felt throughout the sanctuary.

Fallen Soldier

Your funeral program had a handsome picture of you in your uniform, and was filled with family pictures. The order of the service was carefully prepared. Soul-stirring, heartfelt prayers were given; and the choir rendered the melodious tune of "Come let us adore Him."

When we reached the expressions segment of the program which called for expressions of love and reflections, so many people had such nice things to say about you. They spoke of your remarkable, affectionate, gentleman-like characteristics. They talked about your politeness, your demeanor, and the genuine sincere concern you had for your fellow man. Numerous sentiments were expressed describing your unexpected kindness. They attested to your character and the funny things you said as well.

During the program, there were distinguished presentations of the Purple Heart, bronze star, and the American flag. Each was given to Momma and

Farewell to a

Daddy who gracefully accepted them with such pride and sorrow.

Even after the funeral—for ten days actually—the media continued to come to our house including local media from Channel 10, Channel 5, Channel 3, and the *Mobile Press Register*. Representatives from Ft. Lauderdale, FL, California, and even France came to do interviews.

During this time, the United States military testified of your bravery and high standards as a soldier. One of the military officials from Fort Bliss said the barracks where you lived in Fort Bliss will never be the same again, for you blessed them with an everlasting memory. Jessica, one of your comrades, says her life is forever better because of you, and she has gone to school to prepare herself for better things too.

Your untimely demise has left an emptiness that can never be filled.

Fallen Soldier

Grandma used to say, "Sudden death has been a reality since the beginning of time. It is something we must learn to live with, which is much easier said than done."

"How many of our sons and daughters have we flown home in this way through the years in that long line of fallen soldiers? They did not leave a foreign soil looking out the window, seeing the airport lights or the glow of the sinking sun! They never smelled the fumes! They did not feel the quivering as the body of a great plane taxied from the terminal! They never heard the roaring of those massive engines during take-off! Down in the belly of the craft, they never sensed that great blast of power as it picked up speed to leave the ground! Why? Precious and dear, these young Americans heroes were already gone!"

Chuck

Sleep on, Brother, and Take Your Well-Deserved Rest

It was evident during your memorial service how many lives you touched. Though you were only on this earth for what seemed like a brief moment, you left an impact that will last a lifetime—a legacy of kindness, compassion, and love. After your passing, I was determined to not let that legacy die. I went to work and never looked back. These are some of the things we've done to make sure your passing wasn't in vain and to preserve your memory.

In your honor, Momma renamed the center PFC Howard Johnson II Academy & Day Care Center. You always loved working with kids and seeing them grow and develop. Also, in keeping with your desire to help others, the PFC Howard Johnson II Community Development Corporation was established. It is dedicated to paying tuition and providing supplies and uniforms to students who are unable to afford them.

We also had the honor of participating in a ceremony for the re-dedication of a park right around the corner from my house on Cheshire, where we always gather for holidays and special occasions. The city of Mobile and the community as a whole really supported us in our time of loss. Ben Brooks, the city councilman for our district, and Al Stokes, chief of staff for the mayor, said they wanted to name the newly renovated park after you. We got to cut the ribbon as they unveiled the sign for your park at the ceremony. I was so proud. I wish you could have been there.

Daddy was invited to the Unity Missionary Baptist Church to announce a scholarship that was created in your name. He was so proud and touched that you were not forgotten in the El Paso community. You had made a lasting impression there as well—and in such a short amount of time.

Momma was the brainchild of a beverage developed in your name—it's called "Soldier Soda." She even helped to develop the flavor that she named "Grenade," and she helped design the label as well. Sunbelt drinks is test-marketing it right now in Chicago. Not stopping there, Momma was also instrumental in the development of a shoe called PFCHJs that was designed by Tyler Bailey. We were honored that a designer of his magnitude would even consider working with us, but everything turned out so beautiful. I know if you could see it, you would be proud.

March 23, 2013 marks ten years since you left us. We celebrated with a memorial banquet. Our goal was to donate to veterans, the homeless, and those in

Farewell to a

need. We remember how you wanted to help others. It is our desire to do the same and keep your memory a living legacy.

I remember the way you used to bring people over for me to help; I want to reach out the way you did. I want to reach out to the community for every holiday—Valentine's Day, Easter, Memorial Day, Fourth of July, Labor Day, Thanksgiving, and Christmas—and do something for them. I want to make a difference and be visible in the community just like you were.

I don't believe that Momma and Daddy will ever get over your passing. You were their beloved son—Momma's baby, Daddy's boy—the son that they waited 17 years for. It is an unexplainable, indescribable feeling having lost you—a feeling

Fallen Soldier

that soap and water can't take off you. There was nothing that anybody could do to make it right, and no amount of money could bring you back. For many years, I did not understand why you were not here with me. Traditionally, the oldest die first, not the baby.

After you passed, Daddy never stopped. He never missed a Sunday, prayer meeting, choir rehearsal, or board meeting. He maintained all of his civic and social activities. He never missed a beat, and he kept up with the drummer. In the end, it took a toll on him. He experienced full renal failure and, as a result, was required to take dialysis Monday, Wednesday, and Friday with a 5am chair for 4 grueling hours. After years of dialysis due to kidney failure, Daddy received a kidney transplant at age 70. He's still preaching now and will celebrate 31 years as pastor of Truevine on July 2013. Daddy says to tell you that he loves you, misses you, and wishes you

Farewell to a

were here. He welcomes the feeling of your touch on his shoulders as it comes and goes and wants you to know he still goes hunting and loves it.

Daddy asked me to tell you this: "My love for you, Son, will never end. I'll see you someday. My spirit will recognize your spirit, and your spirit will recognize my spirit. What a time when all of God's children get to heaven. Your mother, Gesielle, Quez, Sweetie, Zurich Howard (your namesake), Jack, and Miss Little Sylvia all pass their love on to you. Rest on, my son, rest on. We all loved you, but God loved you more."

Momma is 65 now. After your passing, she buried herself in her work. I always tease her and tell her she's old enough to do the speed limit. She sends all of her love, and she wishes you were here. She talks about you every day, and she still tells everyone that you are her baby. Momma is the director of the PFC Howard Johnson Academy &

Fallen Soldier

Day Care Center, and she hung three huge pictures of you in the entrance to the center. Mom and Dad are working on our new home, as the home on Skywood burned down.

Your sister Selle said to tell you she loves you and misses you too. Your niece Cooter is a sophomore at Bishop State now. She will be graduating next year and going to do her last two years at a university. She still talks about Uncle Junior all the time, and she still remembers the time you bought her those tennis shoes. She still refuses to let anyone else call her Cooter.

Cousin Niesha wants to pass on that she is fine. She has a little girl named Indya Amre who looks just like her, and Indya Amre is her pride and joy. Niesha says she remembers when you would always walk her home from school and make sure she got there okay. She always knew you had her back and remembers when you tried to teach her to fight in

Farewell to a

order to protect herself. It's funny looking back at it, but now she says feels like the heavyweight champion of the world. You're still her hero.

Your nephew Zuke said he misses you too. And he said be sure to tell Grandma thanks for the grits and eggs. Little Joe and Roscoe never had the pleasure of knowing their Uncle Junior, but you can depend on Zuke to tell them about you. Little Joe was named for you—Howard Johnson, Little Joe for short. Little Joe and Roscoe look at your picture, and they wonder about you—what you were like—and they dream about you taking them to the movies and out for ice cream.

And then there is Pie, your bright-eyed, bushy-tailed, round-faced, brown-eyed niece. She walks like a soldier and screams like a commander. You've got to love the Lord for makin' a Pie. She was named after our Grandmom. She is one year old now.

Fallen Soldier

You continue to inspire us every day. We know that despite our loss, we have gained from your life. You were done with the troubles of this world too soon. But troubles don't last always, because God is always standing by. The Bible record is that man is born but a few days, and all of them are full of trouble. You have braved some chilly winds of adversity and climbed some snow-capped mountains of despair. Trials, tribulations and disappointment had the nerve to show up at your door. Even uncertainty had the nerve to show up. With him, he had his sister Doubt, and their cousin Trouble. You answered the door, sent them away, and dared them to come back.

There is no song—there is no place—there are no words to express how I really feel. I think about you every day and long for your touch and your smile. We shared a closeness and brother-sister relationship that was unusual, original, and genuine.

Farewell to a

I will never stop loving you. I will think of you always and of the precious memories of our times and travels. I will always carry you in my mind and heart. It was a plum-pleasing pleasure being your oldest sister. Every moment was the mere essence of sheer delight. I didn't tell you enough how proud I was of you. You were an outstanding, creative, unique, ambitious, enthusiastic individual. You were witty and charming. You were notoriously famous for your biting and satirical wit that kept me laughing and people requested your presence everywhere I went.

Your untimely demise has given me a priceless lesson and an unforgettable experience to put in my suitcase for life. I am your sister; I am your big sister. This is a job that I had worked for 21 years. I was responsible for you. At that moment, without warning or notice, I was dismissed. My sister duties were no longer needed. In your absence, I always asked God to take care of my brother. I finally got

Fallen Soldier

the answer I had been waiting for. God revealed to me what I had asked him for. I asked Him to take care of you, and He did just what I asked him to do. He reminded me that you belong to Him. You were never mine to start with. He just loaned you to me. I thank God for that loan. He relieved me of my sister duties and gave me the blessed assurance that I needed. What a wonderful feeling to have all of my doubts and fears released and suspended. When death came, I was not there when you drew your last breath; but God was. When you realized that you were not going to live, God was there and he took care of you, just like I had asked him to. I could not be there in your time of need, but He was there. He really was, as per my request. He never sleeps, He never takes a nap, He never takes the day off, he never calls in sick, he never takes a vacation, he doesn't have a cell phone, but he is always on the main line. He is on the job 24/7/365. I could never

Farewell to a

repay him for loaning you to me. The interest on this loan is great, and the lender gave me 21 years for the loan to mature.

I thank God for the spirit and kindness that dwelled in you. You have left an indelible mark on my life. I write this letter in living and loving memory of you, my brother, for the unselfish sacrifice you made to your country. Your dedication and loyalty is unsurpassed and second to none. I love you. I honor you, and I celebrate your life, the deeds and accomplishments you achieved before you left.

Thanks to our faith and beliefs, I know I am on my way home too. So tell Saint Peter to open the gate. In the meantime, until I get there, say hello to Grandma and Granddaddy. Tell them I love and miss them more than I could ever tell them. Tell Moses can't wait to see him so we can talk about the Ten Commandments. Tell David, I said he is an awesome Psalmist, tell Job I could use a lesson in patience.

Fallen Soldier

I can just imagine your conversation with Martin and Coretta, Frederick Douglas, Harriet Tubman, Rosa Parks, Matthew, Mark, Luke, John, Timothy, and James. I know that Granny, Grandma, and Aunt Ruby have kissed your jaw countless times already. I know you've seen Sharon and Ken and Uncle Willie D. I'm not worried, for I know you're in good company. I hear that the streets are paved with gold. They tell me the gates to the mansion are made of pearl, and that the upper room has everything fit for a hero.

The wicked shall cease from troubling and weary shall be at rest. Beyond the river I can only imagine what your room must look like. I know it has all the bells and whistles fit for a hero. Have you learned your way around the mansion?

Sleep on, brother, and take your well-deserved rest. From your earthly tasks, you have been properly dismissed, and ordered to rest beyond

Farewell to a Fallen Soldier

the river. Your absence has been excused, and no explanation is necessary, because I know that you are in the presence of the Lord. I commend you for life's race well run and life's work well done. And if the Almighty says "It's alrighty," I'll see you in the morning.

I hope these few lines find you well.

Farewell My Brother,
With All My Love,
Until We Meet Again
Your Big Sister, Quez

"The Salute"

To those who have died,
And to those who have cried.
We Salute You.
To those who have lost,
Paid the ultimate cost.
We Salute You.
And to those who still serve,
The Red White and Blue.
Our grateful Nation,
Proudly Salutes You.

                              Tom Balstad

About the Author

After years of advocacy for families who had lost loved ones, author and entrepreneur Zsaquez "Quez" Johnson lost her own brother when he paid the ultimate sacrifice for his country while serving in Iraq. Fighting the sorrow and loss, she decided to commit her life to helping others in the community. Quez and her extended family reside in Mobile, AL, where she remains determined to carry on her brother's dreams and keep alive his special ability to bring joy and fulfillment to others.

August 27, 2013

Pastor and Mrs. Johnson,

I pray this letter finds you and your family doing well. My name is Octavia Johnson and I am a former member of the Unity Missionary Baptist Church in El Paso Texas where your precious son, Howard Jr served as our drummer. Many years have since passed but I have not forgotten the impact of your son in my life. I think of you all often and pray for you.

I am writing to you because my daughter, Brittany Bullock was the second recipient of the Howard Johnson Memorial Scholarship and I just wanted to say thank you for his sacrifice to this nation and your painful sacrifice as his parents. Brittany went on to graduate from New Mexico State University with a Bachelor's degree in social work and is now serving in the United States Army as well. She is currently stationed at Fort Lee, Virginia. I also have one son who is serving in the Army and he is currently deployed right now in Kuwait.

Again, from the bottom of my heart thank you and although it will not change the ultimate sacrifice that your son gave, I thought that you should know that my daughter did something positive as a result of his scholarship. May God continue to bless you and your entire family.

Octavia Johnson

www.ingramcontent.com/pod-product-compliance
Lightning Source LLC
Chambersburg PA
CBHW020659300426
44112CB00007B/455